JOSH STEVE

AI Investor's Suspenseful Handbook

Copyright © 2023 by Josh Steve

All rights reserved. No part of this publication may be reproduced, stored or transmitted in any form or by any means, electronic, mechanical, photocopying, recording, scanning, or otherwise without written permission from the publisher. It is illegal to copy this book, post it to a website, or distribute it by any other means without permission.

This novel is entirely a work of fiction. The names, characters and incidents portrayed in it are the work of the author's imagination. Any resemblance to actual persons, living or dead, events or localities is entirely coincidental.

Josh Steve asserts the moral right to be identified as the author of this work.

First edition

This book was professionally typeset on Reedsy.
Find out more at reedsy.com

Contents

The Hidden Opportunity	1
Uncovering the Enigma	4
The Whisper Network	7
Cracks in the Facade	12
The Race to Decode	16
Behind Closed Doors	20
The Tipping Point	24
Unmasking the Enigma	28
The Revelation	32
The Final Confrontation	36
The Aftermath	42
Operation Phoenix Rising	46

The Hidden Opportunity

The New York City skyline shimmered beneath a twilight sky, casting long shadows over the bustling streets below. In the heart of the financial district, where glass-and-steel towers reached for the heavens, the world of high finance thrived. Among the suits and ties, and the ever-present aroma of ambition, an enigma was quietly taking shape.

Jason Reeves, a talented but overlooked portfolio manager, had spent years navigating the labyrinthine pathways of Wall Street. He'd earned his stripes crunching numbers, analyzing trends, and playing the risky game of investing. Yet, the rumors he'd heard lately were unlike anything he'd ever encountered.

As Jason sat in his dimly lit office, surrounded by charts and stock tickers, a hushed conversation drifted through the office walls like a seductive whisper. Colleagues spoke of a mysterious AI-driven stock that was outperforming everything else, consistently and inexplicably. The details were scant, shrouded in secrecy, and veiled in intrigue.

This was not the first time Jason had heard whispers of a hidden opportunity in the cutthroat world of finance. But this felt different. This felt like the elusive unicorn he'd been chasing his entire career.

His curiosity piqued, Jason began to dig deeper. He tapped into his network, connected with old acquaintances, and exchanged cryptic messages with a source he'd rather not name. It was a clandestine journey through the digital underbelly of financial information, where secrets were traded like currency.

The more he uncovered, the more he realized that this AI stock was unlike any other investment opportunity he'd encountered. It was a puzzle that had yet to be solved, a secret that had yet to be revealed. What intrigued him most was the consistency of its returns. The AI stock seemed to possess a supernatural ability to predict market movements with pinpoint accuracy.

Jason's initial skepticism transformed into a burning desire to understand the mechanics behind this AI's uncanny success. His nights became consumed by research, his days by relentless pursuit. He sought out experts in artificial intelligence, poring over technical papers and dissecting algorithms. But each lead led him down a winding path that grew darker and more labyrinthine with every step.

One evening, as a rainstorm drenched the city in an unrelenting downpour, Jason's breakthrough came. He stumbled upon a small, inconspicuous forum buried deep in the recesses of the internet. It was a haven for data scientists, quants, and those who dared to venture beyond the conventional boundaries of investing.

In a thread titled "The AI Enigma," a user named Cipher42 shared tantalizing breadcrumbs of information. It was here that Jason found the first glimmers of hope in unraveling the AI's secrets. Cipher42, it seemed, was on a similar quest, driven by a relentless curiosity that mirrored Jason's own.

Cryptic messages flowed between the two, exchanged under the veil of anonymity. They spoke in riddles, danced around the specifics, and alluded to the AI's immense potential. Jason learned that Cipher42 was, in fact, a data scientist with a deep passion for unraveling the mysteries of machine intelligence. Their shared obsession united them in an unspoken pact to break through the walls of secrecy surrounding the AI stock.

THE HIDDEN OPPORTUNITY

Days turned into weeks, and Jason's obsession grew. He began to piece together the fragments of information he'd collected from Cipher42 and other sources. It was as though he were assembling a jigsaw puzzle with no picture to guide him. Each revelation only deepened the mystery.

It was during one particularly sleepless night that Jason received an encrypted message from Cipher42, signaling a potential breakthrough. The message contained a complex algorithm, a digital key that could unlock the AI's inner workings. But there was a catch – deciphering it would require a level of expertise that went beyond Jason's skillset.

The city outside his window was cloaked in darkness, and the distant sound of sirens seemed to underscore the gravity of the moment. Jason was standing at the precipice of something monumental, something that could either catapult his career to unimaginable heights or lead him to financial ruin.

The rain had ceased, and a pale moon hung low in the sky, casting eerie shadows across Jason's office. He stared at the screen, the cursor blinking rhythmically beside Cipher42's message. The choice was his: to dive deeper into the abyss of uncertainty or to walk away, forever haunted by the enigma that had consumed his thoughts.

With trembling fingers, Jason made his decision. He would embark on a perilous journey into the world of artificial intelligence, where secrets were guarded fiercely, and the line between brilliance and madness blurred. The hidden opportunity beckoned, and he couldn't resist its siren call.

As the first rays of dawn broke through the city's skyline, Jason began his quest to decipher the AI's algorithm, unaware of the dangers and revelations that awaited him in the pursuit of the elusive AI-driven stock.

Uncovering the Enigma

The days grew shorter, and autumn's chill settled over New York City as Jason Reeves delved deeper into the enigma of the AI-driven stock. With Cipher42's algorithm as his guiding star, he embarked on a quest that would lead him through the labyrinthine history of artificial intelligence in the world of finance.

In his pursuit of knowledge, Jason unearthed a trail of breadcrumbs that stretched back decades. It all began in the late 1980s, when Wall Street first toyed with the idea of using computers to predict market movements. Jason's research took him to a dimly lit basement in the heart of Manhattan, where a group of renegade computer scientists had gathered to change the world.

The room was filled with the hum of ancient mainframes and the clatter of mechanical keyboards. Graffiti-covered walls bore witness to the counter-culture spirit that had birthed the digital revolution. It was here that Jason met an eccentric figure named Dr. Edwin Holloway, a brilliant but reclusive computer scientist with a shock of unruly white hair and eyes that sparkled with manic intensity.

Dr. Holloway, it turned out, had been a pioneer in the field of artificial intelligence. In a time when most scoffed at the idea of machines predicting financial markets, he had dared to dream differently. He believed that the chaos of Wall Street could be tamed by the precision of algorithms.

Jason sat across from Dr. Holloway in a cluttered office adorned with circuit diagrams and equations scrawled on chalkboards. The air was thick with the smell of old books and the faint whirring of computer fans. Jason had expected to find a mad scientist, but what he encountered was a visionary who had been ahead of his time.

The old man leaned in, his voice a conspiratorial whisper. "You're on the trail, young man," he said, his eyes glittering with a mixture of excitement and nostalgia. "The AI you're chasing, it has roots that run deep. I was there when it all began."

Jason listened intently as Dr. Holloway recounted the early days of AI experimentation on Wall Street. It was a time when computers were seen as tools for automation, not intelligence. But Dr. Holloway and his band of misfit geniuses believed otherwise. They saw the potential for machines to analyze vast datasets and make predictions that no human mind could fathom.

As Dr. Holloway spoke, Jason realized that he had stumbled upon a hidden chapter in the history of finance. The pioneers of AI investing had been rebels, scoffed at by their peers, and ostracized by the establishment. They had worked in secrecy, driven by a fervent belief in the power of algorithms.

The story took a darker turn when Dr. Holloway revealed that their groundbreaking work had caught the attention of powerful interests. "They wanted what we had," he said cryptically, his eyes narrowing. "They wanted to control the future of finance."

Jason pressed for more details, but Dr. Holloway grew evasive. He warned Jason that he was treading on dangerous ground, that the secrets of AI investing were guarded by powerful forces willing to protect them at any cost.

The encounter left Jason with more questions than answers. He had glimpsed a hidden world of AI experimentation on Wall Street, but the true nature of the AI-driven stock remained elusive. The pieces of the puzzle were scattered, and he needed more than history to solve it.

Days turned into weeks as Jason continued his research. He discovered that the history of AI in finance was a patchwork of failed experiments, abandoned projects, and the occasional breakthrough. The technology had evolved, but the secrets of its success remained well-guarded.

One evening, as the city lights sparkled below, Jason received another message from Cipher42. It contained a tantalizing clue: a name, Dr. Mariana Valentina, a renowned AI researcher with a reputation for pushing the boundaries of machine intelligence.

It seemed that Dr. Valentina had recently made a breakthrough in AI forecasting that was causing ripples in the financial world. Rumors suggested that her work might be linked to the mysterious AI stock. Jason knew he had to find her, to uncover the truth behind the enigma.

With the name as his only lead, he embarked on a journey to track down Dr. Mariana Valentina, a brilliant mind whose discoveries held the key to unraveling the AI's secrets. Little did he know that this quest would lead him deeper into the shadows of Wall Street, where danger and deception lurked at every turn.

The next chapter of his journey awaited, and Jason was prepared to follow the trail wherever it led, even if it meant confronting the powerful forces determined to keep the AI's secrets hidden. The enigma of the AI-driven stock was drawing him in, and he couldn't turn back now.

The Whisper Network

The city lights danced below as Jason Reeves stood on the rooftop of a nondescript office building. The chill of the night air cut through his coat, but he paid it no mind. He was on the cusp of a breakthrough, and every fiber of his being hummed with anticipation.

His search for Dr. Mariana Valentina had taken him to the heart of Manhattan's academic elite. She was a professor at the prestigious New York Institute of Technology, known for her groundbreaking work in artificial intelligence. But Jason wasn't here for a casual interview. He needed answers, and he was willing to go to great lengths to get them.

The university's campus was a blend of modern architecture and ivy-covered tradition. As Jason walked through the hallowed halls, he couldn't shake the feeling that he was entering a realm where secrets were traded like currency. He had arranged a meeting with Dr. Valentina under the guise of a journalist interested in her research, but he knew that the truth he sought was far more elusive.

The meeting took place in her cluttered office, where stacks of research papers teetered precariously, and a whiteboard bore a maze of equations. Dr. Valentina herself was a woman in her late forties, with piercing green eyes that seemed to size up Jason the moment he entered. Her hair, a cascade of unruly black curls, framed a face marked by the lines of relentless inquiry.

"Mr. Reeves," she said, extending a hand as he entered. Her handshake was firm, her gaze unyielding. "I understand you're interested in my work."

Jason nodded, choosing his words carefully. "Your recent breakthroughs in AI forecasting have garnered a lot of attention in financial circles. I'm intrigued by the potential applications of your research."

Dr. Valentina's eyes flickered with curiosity. "I've had my share of inquiries from investors," she said, her tone measured. "But my research is still in its early stages. The true potential is yet to be unlocked."

Jason pressed further, his questions veiled in the guise of journalistic curiosity. He asked about her methodology, her datasets, and the algorithms she employed. Dr. Valentina answered with a scientist's precision, revealing just enough to pique his interest but not enough to satisfy his hunger for knowledge.

As the interview progressed, Jason sensed that there was more to Dr. Valentina's work than met the eye. She hinted at a "whisper network" of data scientists, quants, and academics who shared their findings in the shadows of the financial world. It was a world where information flowed like a clandestine river, and those who possessed it held immense power.

Jason probed further, asking about the AI-driven stock without mentioning it by name. Dr. Valentina's demeanor shifted, and her eyes took on a guarded look. "I'm aware of the stock you're referring to," she said carefully. "But I have no direct involvement with it. My research is purely academic."

The ambiguity in her response only deepened Jason's suspicion. He knew that the AI stock was somehow connected to her work, and he was determined to uncover the truth. But Dr. Valentina was no ordinary interview subject.

She was a formidable intellect, and her evasiveness was a testament to the secrecy surrounding the AI's origins.

The meeting concluded with a promise to stay in touch, but Jason left Dr. Valentina's office with more questions than answers. He needed to dig deeper, to penetrate the elusive "whisper network" she had alluded to. It was clear that the key to unraveling the enigma of the AI-driven stock lay in the shadows of this clandestine world.

Over the following weeks, Jason immersed himself in the underground network of data scientists and quants who traded information like currency. He adopted a new identity, a persona of a tech-savvy investor seeking an edge in the market. He frequented online forums, attended secretive meetups, and engaged in encrypted conversations.

It was in the darkest corners of the internet that he discovered the existence of a select group known as "The Syndicate." These were the insiders, the gatekeepers of the AI's secrets. They operated with ruthless efficiency, guarding their knowledge with the zeal of a secret society.

Jason's pursuit led him to a clandestine online forum where members of The Syndicate exchanged information and discussed the AI-driven stock. It was a digital underworld where pseudonyms and encrypted channels shielded their identities. The chatter was cryptic, filled with acronyms and coded language that only insiders could decipher.

As Jason delved deeper into the forum, he realized that he was not alone in his quest. Others, like him, were drawn to the allure of the AI-driven stock. They traded tips, shared theories, and debated its true origins. But The Syndicate remained elusive, a shadowy presence that pulled the strings from the darkness.

One evening, as Jason scoured the forum for clues, he received a private message from an anonymous user with the handle "Whisperer." The message was short and cryptic: "Meet me. Tomorrow. Midnight. The abandoned subway station beneath Chambers Street. Come alone."

The hairs on the back of Jason's neck stood on end. He had stumbled upon a lead, an opportunity to get closer to The Syndicate. But the rendezvous in the abandoned subway station carried an air of danger and intrigue. He knew he was stepping into the unknown, but the enigma of the AI-driven stock beckoned him forward.

As the clock ticked towards midnight, Jason stood on the deserted platform of the Chambers Street subway station, shrouded in darkness and uncertainty. The station had been abandoned for years, its tunnels echoing with the ghosts of a bygone era. It was a fitting backdrop for a meeting that could change everything.

Minutes stretched into eternity, and just as doubt began to creep in, a figure emerged from the shadows. The Whisperer was a silhouette, a spectral presence that seemed to materialize out of thin air. Their voice was a low, modulated whisper that sent shivers down Jason's spine.

"You seek answers," the Whisperer said, their words tinged with mystery. "But the path you tread is treacherous. The Syndicate guards its secrets with ferocity."

Jason nodded, his pulse quickening with anticipation. "I need to know about the AI-driven stock, about its origins, and the power that lies behind it."

The Whisperer hesitated, as though weighing the consequences of revealing too much. "The Syndicate is a network of the elite, the privileged few who have harnessed the power of artificial intelligence to manipulate markets. They control the AI stock, and their reach extends far beyond Wall Street."

Jason's mind raced with possibilities. The Syndicate was the key, the gatekeepers of the AI's secrets. But how could he penetrate their ranks? How could he unravel the enigma without falling victim to its dangers?

The Whisperer leaned closer, their face hidden in the shadows. "To gain access to The Syndicate, you must prove your worth. You must demonstrate your commitment to the cause."

Jason's heart pounded in his chest. The Whisperer's words held the promise of answers, but they also carried an ominous warning. The path ahead was perilous, and the dangers were real. Yet, the enigma of the AI-driven stock beckoned him forward, and he knew there was no turning back.

The stage was

set for a high-stakes gamble, a journey that would test Jason's resolve and push him to the limits of his courage. The secrets of The Syndicate awaited, shrouded in the darkness of the underground world where whispers held more power than words. Jason had made a choice, and the consequences would be dire or enlightening.

Cracks in the Facade

The city that never slept was a maze of shadows as Jason Reeves navigated its labyrinthine streets. He was on the precipice of a decision that would determine his fate. The Whisperer's words still echoed in his mind, and the path ahead was fraught with danger.

To prove his worth to The Syndicate, Jason needed to demonstrate his commitment to the cause. The message from the Whisperer had been clear: "Find the Crack in the Facade." It was a cryptic directive that held the key to gaining access to the enigmatic world of AI-driven stocks.

The phrase had haunted Jason's thoughts, and he had scoured the depths of the internet, searching for clues. It was during one sleepless night that he stumbled upon a thread in an obscure online forum. The thread's title was "Cracks in the Facade: Unmasking the AI Masters," and it promised revelations that bordered on the surreal.

As he delved into the thread, Jason found himself in the company of conspiracy theorists, whistleblowers, and those who believed that the financial world was a carefully constructed illusion. The thread was a treasure trove of theories, speculations, and stories of market manipulation that defied explanation.

One user, who went by the alias "FacadeBreaker," claimed to have insider knowledge of The Syndicate's operations. He described a world where AI algorithms controlled the ebb and flow of financial markets, where fortunes were made and lost in the blink of an eye. According to FacadeBreaker, The Syndicate operated with a ruthless efficiency that left no room for error.

But it was one specific post that caught Jason's attention. A user named "CipheredHeart" had left a comment, hinting at a hidden vulnerability within The Syndicate's operations. It was a slender thread of hope in a web of uncertainty.

Jason reached out to CipheredHeart, engaging in a coded exchange that revealed little but hinted at a shared objective. The message culminated in a cryptic invitation: "Meet me. Midnight. The abandoned subway station beneath Chambers Street."

The choice was clear, and the echoes of his previous rendezvous with the Whisperer only added to the sense of foreboding. The Chambers Street subway station had become a nexus of intrigue, a place where secrets were exchanged in the darkness.

As the appointed hour approached, Jason descended into the abandoned station once more. The subterranean world was a place of eerie silence, broken only by the distant rumble of subway trains on neighboring tracks. Graffiti-covered walls bore witness to the passage of time, and the air was heavy with the weight of history.

He stood alone on the platform, his senses heightened by a potent mix of anticipation and fear. Moments stretched into an eternity, and just when doubt threatened to overpower resolve, a figure emerged from the shadows.

CipheredHeart was a spectral presence, their identity concealed beneath layers of clothing and a mask that obscured their face. Their voice was a low, modulated whisper, and the words carried a weight that belied their enigmatic nature.

"You seek the Crack in the Facade," CipheredHeart said, their tone tinged with a sense of urgency. "It is a weakness in The Syndicate's operations, a vulnerability that can be exploited."

Jason nodded, his pulse quickening with anticipation. "Tell me more. How do I find it?"

CipheredHeart hesitated, their eyes hidden behind the mask. "The Crack lies in the hidden algorithms that drive the AI's predictions. They are a double-edged sword, powerful but fragile. There is a way to disrupt them, to unmask the true nature of The Syndicate's control."

The revelation sent a shiver down Jason's spine. The algorithms, the very heart of The Syndicate's power, held the key to unraveling the enigma. But the path to exploiting their vulnerability was treacherous, and the consequences of failure were dire.

CipheredHeart continued, their words laced with caution. "To access the algorithms, you must infiltrate The Syndicate's inner circle. They guard their secrets fiercely, and trust is a rare commodity. You will need to earn their confidence, to become one of them."

The weight of the task ahead bore down on Jason. Infiltrating The Syndicate was no small feat, and the risks were staggering. But the allure of exposing the truth, of unmasking the power behind the AI-driven stock, was an irresistible force.

CipheredHeart's voice grew solemn. "Remember, the path to the Crack is perilous. The Syndicate will test you, scrutinize your every move. But if you succeed, you will gain access to the algorithms and the knowledge that lies at the heart of their operation."

With those words, CipheredHeart disappeared into the shadows, leaving

Jason alone in the abandoned subway station. The path ahead was clear, but the challenges were daunting. He knew that he was about to embark on a journey that would push him to his limits, a journey that could either expose the enigma or lead to his downfall.

The city outside was a cacophony of lights and noise, but in the depths of the underground, Jason's world had narrowed to a singular purpose: finding the Crack in the Facade, infiltrating The Syndicate, and unraveling the secrets that lay hidden within the algorithms. The enigma of the AI-driven stock beckoned him forward, and there was no turning back now.

The Race to Decode

As Jason Reeves delved deeper into the enigma of the AI-driven stock, he found himself consumed by a relentless quest for knowledge. The path ahead was fraught with danger, but the allure of unraveling the secrets hidden within the algorithms was an irresistible force.

The city's heartbeat pulsed around him as he walked through its neon-lit streets. Jason had spent weeks researching The Syndicate and their elusive inner circle. He had adopted a new identity, a persona of an ambitious tech investor, and had begun to infiltrate the world of secretive financial meetups and clandestine gatherings.

His efforts had not gone unnoticed. Whispers of the newcomer who sought to gain access to The Syndicate's inner sanctum had spread through the underground channels of the financial world. Jason was being scrutinized, tested for his commitment and resourcefulness.

One evening, as he attended a covert gathering in a dimly lit speakeasy, he was approached by a woman named Lydia, a formidable presence with sharp eyes that seemed to pierce through his façade. She was a member of The Syndicate's outer circle, a gatekeeper to the inner sanctum.

Lydia's voice was a low, measured whisper as she spoke. "You seek something,

Mr. Reeves," she said, her gaze unwavering. "But what are you willing to do to obtain it?"

Jason had prepared for this moment, and his response was carefully calculated. "I'm willing to invest not only my resources but my knowledge and expertise. I believe in the power of AI, and I want to contribute to The Syndicate's cause."

Lydia nodded, her expression inscrutable. "The path ahead is treacherous. The Syndicate demands loyalty, discretion, and above all, results. To gain access to the inner circle, you must prove your worth."

She handed him an encrypted USB drive and a slip of paper with an address. "Tomorrow night, you will go to this location. You will meet with a contact who will provide you with a task. Complete it, and you will have taken the first step toward earning our trust."

Jason accepted the USB drive and the address, his heart pounding with a mixture of excitement and apprehension. The moment of truth was approaching, and the challenges ahead were unknown.

The meeting concluded, and Jason left the speakeasy, his mind racing with questions. What task awaited him at the specified location? How could he prove himself to The Syndicate without revealing his true objective—to expose the secrets of the AI-driven stock?

The following night, Jason arrived at the address, a nondescript warehouse on the outskirts of the city. The area was cloaked in darkness, and the only source of light emanated from a small side entrance. He hesitated for a moment, his breath visible in the cold night air, before entering the dimly lit interior.

Inside, he found himself in a makeshift tech lab, where screens displayed lines of code and data streams. A figure clad in a hoodie and obscured by shadows stood before a bank of computers. The contact.

Without a word, the contact handed Jason a folder containing a dossier of financial data, market trends, and stock predictions. "Your task is to analyze this data," the contact said, their voice digitally distorted. "Identify patterns, anomalies, anything that could give us an edge in the market. The Syndicate values those who can interpret the language of numbers."

Jason accepted the folder, his mind racing with possibilities. This was his chance to gain The Syndicate's trust, to get closer to the algorithms that held the key to the AI-driven stock's secrets.

Days turned into weeks as Jason immersed himself in the data. He worked tirelessly, his determination unwavering. He began to notice subtle patterns in the market trends, irregularities that hinted at the presence of a hidden hand. It was as though the AI-driven stock left a digital fingerprint, a trace of its manipulation.

But the deeper he delved, the more he realized that he was not alone in his pursuit. Other members of The Syndicate were also analyzing the data, each seeking to uncover the same secrets. The competition was fierce, and the stakes were high.

One evening, as he pored over the data in his dimly lit apartment, Jason received an anonymous message on his encrypted communication channel. It contained a simple yet chilling warning: "You're being watched."

The message sent a shiver down his spine. The Syndicate was aware of his activities, and his every move was being scrutinized. He had entered a high-stakes race to decode the AI's secrets, a race where the consequences of failure were unknown.

Doubt gnawed at the edges of his resolve, but he couldn't turn back now. The enigma of the AI-driven stock held him in its grip, and the desire to expose the truth was a fire that burned within him.

As the days passed, Jason's analysis of the data deepened. He began to suspect that The Syndicate's manipulation of the stock was not as flawless as it seemed. There were cracks in the facade, subtle imperfections that revealed vulnerabilities in the algorithms.

One night, as he uncovered a particularly telling pattern, he received another message, this time from Lydia. It contained a location and a time—a clandestine meeting with The Syndicate's inner circle.

The opportunity was unprecedented, and the risks were monumental. Jason knew that the enigma of the AI-driven stock was drawing him into a web of intrigue and danger. The race to decode the algorithms was reaching its climax, and the moment of truth was fast approaching.

With the folder of data in hand and the weight of his discoveries on his shoulders, Jason prepared to meet with The Syndicate's inner circle, to prove his worth, and to get one step closer to the secrets that lay hidden within the algorithms. The city outside was a blur of lights and shadows, but in the world he had entered, the lines between reality and illusion had blurred, and the enigma of the AI-driven stock held him in its relentless grip.

Behind Closed Doors

The night was moonless as Jason Reeves stood before the address he had received from Lydia. It was a location shrouded in secrecy, a penthouse atop one of the city's towering skyscrapers. The city below pulsed with life, but here, in the shadows of the financial district, a different world awaited.

With each step he took toward the penthouse, the weight of the folder containing his analysis grew heavier. He knew that the meeting with The Syndicate's inner circle was a pivotal moment, a chance to prove himself and gain access to the elusive algorithms behind the AI-driven stock.

As the elevator ascended, he couldn't help but wonder who comprised this inner circle. What kind of power and influence did they hold over the financial world? And what secrets did they possess about the AI's true capabilities?

The elevator doors opened to reveal a luxurious penthouse bathed in soft, dim light. The room was adorned with modern art and sleek furnishings, a stark contrast to the world of data and algorithms Jason had inhabited for weeks. At the center of the room, a long glass table held a group of individuals who turned their gaze toward him as he entered.

Lydia, her sharp eyes still piercing, was among them. She gestured for Jason to take a seat at the head of the table, where a leather-bound dossier awaited him. The members of The Syndicate remained silent, their identities hidden behind masks of calm and reserve.

Jason's heart pounded in his chest as he opened the dossier. Inside, he found a series of financial reports, market analyses, and stock predictions, all bearing The Syndicate's unmistakable signature. The task was clear—to analyze the data and uncover any hidden insights that could give The Syndicate an edge in the market.

Time seemed to blur as Jason delved into the data. He scanned lines of numbers and charts, searching for anomalies and patterns that would reveal the AI's secrets. The room was a hushed sanctuary of anticipation, and the weight of expectation hung in the air.

Hours passed, and the world beyond the penthouse faded into obscurity. Jason's focus was laser-sharp as he uncovered subtle irregularities in the market trends. It was as though the AI-driven stock left behind a digital trail, a breadcrumb trail of its manipulation.

As he presented his findings to The Syndicate, the room remained silent, their masked expressions inscrutable. He could feel their scrutiny, their judgment, as they absorbed his analysis. The stakes were impossibly high, and the outcome of this meeting would shape his fate.

Finally, one member of The Syndicate, a figure shrouded in darkness, spoke. "Your analysis is intriguing, Mr. Reeves," they said, their voice betraying nothing. "But it is only the beginning. The Syndicate values those who can see beyond the surface, who can decipher the language of the market."

The words were cryptic, and Jason knew that he had passed a test, but the path ahead was far from clear. The Syndicate demanded more, and the enigma of the AI-driven stock held its secrets tightly.

Lydia leaned in, her voice a whisper in the stillness of the room. "To gain access to the inner circle, you must demonstrate your commitment to The Syndicate's cause. You must prove that you are willing to do whatever it takes to maintain the balance of power."

The message was clear—Jason's journey was far from over. The Syndicate's inner circle held the key to the algorithms, and he would need to earn their trust to get closer to the truth.

In the days that followed, Jason delved deeper into the world of The Syndicate, attending secret meetings, analyzing market data, and honing his skills as a financial operative. He became entangled in a web of intrigue and power, where allegiances shifted like quicksilver and the line between ally and adversary blurred.

It was during one late-night meeting in a dimly lit office that he encountered a figure who would change the course of his journey. The man's name was Max Donovan, a former member of The Syndicate's inner circle who had grown disillusioned with their control over the financial world.

Max revealed that The Syndicate was not just a group of investors seeking profit but an organization with a grander vision—to manipulate global markets and shape the course of economies. He spoke of a hidden agenda, a plan to use the AI-driven stock to exert control over governments and institutions.

Jason's shock was palpable. The AI-driven stock was not just a tool for profit; it was a weapon in a covert war for financial supremacy. The Syndicate's ambitions were far-reaching, and the consequences of their actions could reshape the world.

Max offered Jason a choice—to continue down the path of The Syndicate, with its allure of power and wealth, or to join him in a mission to expose the truth, to unmask the enigma of the AI-driven stock and bring its manipulators to justice.

It was a decision that would define Jason's destiny. The city's heartbeat pulsed around him as he stood at the crossroads of power and integrity, of ambition and justice. The enigma of the AI-driven stock held him in its relentless grip, and the world of shadows and secrets beckoned him forward.

As he contemplated his choice, Jason couldn't help but wonder what lay behind the closed doors of The Syndicate's inner circle. The algorithms held the key to the AI's secrets, but the journey to unlock them was treacherous, and the dangers that lurked in the shadows were real.

The Tipping Point

The city was alive with a cacophony of sounds and lights as Jason Reeves stood on the precipice of a life-altering decision. Max Donovan's revelations about The Syndicate's true ambitions had shaken him to his core. The AI-driven stock was not just a tool for profit; it was a weapon in a covert war for financial supremacy. The consequences of their actions could reshape the world.

Max had offered Jason a choice—to continue down the path of The Syndicate, with its allure of power and wealth, or to join him in a mission to expose the truth and bring the manipulators of the AI-driven stock to justice.

As Jason weighed his options, he knew that he was standing at a crossroads. The allure of power and wealth held its seductive grip, but the ideals of justice and integrity tugged at his conscience. The enigma of the AI-driven stock had led him on a treacherous journey, and the path ahead was uncertain.

In the days that followed, Jason delved deeper into Max's world, learning about the underground network of whistleblowers, investigators, and journalists who were dedicated to exposing The Syndicate's secrets. It was a world where truth was a precious commodity, and the risks were immeasurable.

THE TIPPING POINT

Max introduced Jason to a brilliant investigative journalist named Sarah Reynolds. She had spent years uncovering the trail of financial manipulation and corporate espionage that led to The Syndicate. Her research had unearthed a web of deceit that spanned governments and institutions, a web that The Syndicate had woven with meticulous precision.

Sarah's determination and courage were infectious, and Jason felt drawn to her cause. Together, they embarked on a mission to expose The Syndicate's true agenda and unmask the enigma of the AI-driven stock. Their journey would take them to the darkest corners of the financial world, where danger lurked at every turn.

Their first breakthrough came in the form of a leak—an anonymous source within The Syndicate had provided Sarah with a trove of confidential documents and correspondence. It was a treasure trove of information that offered a glimpse into the inner workings of the secretive organization.

The documents revealed a chilling truth. The Syndicate had manipulated financial markets on a global scale, orchestrating crises and profiting from the chaos they created. Their ambitions extended beyond Wall Street, with plans to control governments, economies, and the fate of nations.

As Jason and Sarah delved deeper into the documents, they uncovered evidence of a sinister plot known as "Project Phoenix." It was a plan to use the AI-driven stock to destabilize the global economy and reshape it in The Syndicate's image. The consequences of Project Phoenix were catastrophic, and the world remained oblivious to the impending threat.

With their evidence in hand, Jason and Sarah knew that they had a duty to expose The Syndicate's true agenda. They would need to bypass the powerful interests that protected The Syndicate and bring their findings to the world's attention.

Their journey took them to a hidden network of activists and hackers who shared their mission. These digital warriors possessed the skills and knowledge to breach The Syndicate's defenses and reveal the truth to the world. It was a risky endeavor, and the consequences of failure were dire.

The plan was set in motion—a coordinated cyberattack that would expose The Syndicate's secrets to the world. As Jason and Sarah watched from the shadows, the hackers infiltrated The Syndicate's systems, bypassing firewalls and encryption barriers.

The clock ticked down, and tension hung in the air as the hackers worked tirelessly to extract the incriminating data. It was a race against time, with The Syndicate's defenses closing in. Jason and Sarah's hearts pounded in their chests as they watched the progress bar inch closer to completion.

Finally, it was done—the data was secure, and The Syndicate's secrets were in their possession. But the victory was short-lived. The Syndicate had detected the breach and was closing in on their location.

With the stolen data in hand, Jason and Sarah fled through a labyrinthine network of tunnels and hidden passages, pursued by unseen adversaries. The world outside was a blur of lights and shadows as they raced against time to reach safety.

Their journey took them to an underground safehouse, a hidden refuge where activists and whistleblowers gathered to expose corruption and injustice. It was a place of anonymity and security, a sanctuary for those who dared to challenge the status quo.

As they examined the stolen data, Jason and Sarah realized the magnitude of their discovery. The evidence against The Syndicate was irrefutable, a damning exposé of their manipulation and deceit. But the battle was far from over.

The enigma of the AI-driven stock had drawn Jason into a world of intrigue and danger, a world where truth and justice hung in the balance. The consequences of their actions were uncertain, and the forces that protected The Syndicate were formidable.

But Jason and Sarah were determined to see their mission through, to expose the truth and bring The Syndicate to justice. The enigma had led them to this pivotal moment, a moment that would test their resolve and reshape the fate of the financial world.

As they prepared to release the stolen data to the world, they knew that they were standing on the precipice of history. The enigma of the AI-driven stock had brought them to the tipping point, and the world would soon know the truth that had remained hidden for far too long.

Unmasking the Enigma

The underground safehouse was alive with tension as Jason Reeves and Sarah Reynolds prepared to expose The Syndicate's secrets to the world. The stolen data, a damning exposé of financial manipulation and deceit, was their weapon. But with great power came great risk, and the consequences of their actions were uncertain.

As they stood before a bank of computers, their fingers poised over the keyboard, Jason and Sarah knew that they were about to embark on a journey that would change the course of history. The enigma of the AI-driven stock had drawn them into a world of intrigue and danger, and the time had come to unmask the hidden manipulators.

With a deep breath, Jason initiated the upload. Lines of code streamed across the screen as the stolen data was transmitted to servers around the world. The information was encrypted, protected by layers of security, but The Syndicate would not be far behind.

As the progress bar inched forward, Sarah monitored incoming messages on a secure communication channel. It didn't take long for the first warning to arrive—a cryptic message from an anonymous source.

"They're onto us. Get out now."

The message sent a jolt of adrenaline through Jason and Sarah. The Syndicate had detected the breach, and their defenses were closing in. The safehouse, once a sanctuary, had become a trap.

With a sense of urgency, they disconnected from the computers and began to gather their belongings. The clock was ticking, and escape was their only option.

As they made their way through the winding tunnels of the safehouse, a distant sound of footsteps echoed behind them. The pursuers were closing in, and the shadows seemed to shift with every passing moment.

They emerged into the dimly lit streets of the city, their breath visible in the frigid night air. The world outside was a blur of lights and shadows as they raced against time to reach safety. But The Syndicate's reach extended far beyond Wall Street, and the dangers that lurked in the darkness were real.

Jason and Sarah's path took them to a network of safehouses and allies who had dedicated their lives to exposing corruption and injustice. These underground activists were their only hope, their last line of defense against The Syndicate's relentless pursuit.

Hours turned into days as they moved from one safehouse to another, always one step ahead of their adversaries. The stolen data had reverberated through the financial world, sending shockwaves of panic and uncertainty. The world was watching, waiting for the truth to be revealed.

But The Syndicate was not about to give up without a fight. They unleashed a relentless campaign of disinformation and propaganda, painting Jason and Sarah as rogue operatives seeking to undermine the global economy. The world was divided, and the battle for truth had become a war of narratives.

As Jason and Sarah navigated the treacherous waters of deception and manipulation, they received a cryptic message from an anonymous source—a whistleblower within The Syndicate who had grown disillusioned with their actions. The source offered to meet in person, to provide them with information that could expose the enigma of the AI-driven stock once and for all.

The meeting took place in the dead of night, in a clandestine location on the outskirts of the city. The source was a shadowy figure whose identity remained hidden behind layers of disguise. Their voice was a whisper in the darkness, and their words carried the weight of revelation.

"The AI-driven stock is just the tip of the iceberg," the source said, their voice tinged with urgency. "The Syndicate's true agenda goes much deeper. They seek to control not only financial markets but governments and institutions. They have infiltrated the highest levels of power, and their influence extends far beyond Wall Street."

Jason and Sarah listened in awe as the source revealed a hidden world of corporate espionage, political manipulation, and economic warfare. The Syndicate's ambitions were boundless, and the consequences of their actions could reshape the fate of nations.

But the source had a revelation that would send shockwaves through the financial world. They possessed evidence of The Syndicate's involvement in Project Phoenix—a plan to use the AI-driven stock to destabilize the global economy and reshape it in their image.

With this evidence in their possession, Jason and Sarah knew that they had the key to unmasking the enigma of the AI-driven stock. The battle for truth had reached its climax, and the world awaited their next move.

As they prepared to release the evidence to the world, they were acutely aware of the risks they faced. The Syndicate would stop at nothing to protect their secrets, and the consequences of their actions were unpredictable.

But the enigma of the AI-driven stock had led them on a journey of discovery and revelation, a journey that had tested their resolve and pushed them to the limits of their courage. The truth was within their grasp, and they were determined to see their mission through to the end, to expose The Syndicate's true agenda and bring its manipulators to justice.

With the evidence in hand, Jason and Sarah initiated the release. The information would be broadcast to the world, unmasking The Syndicate's secrets and revealing the extent of their manipulation. The consequences would be far-reaching, and the world would soon know the truth that had remained hidden for far too long.

As they watched the progress bar inch forward, a sense of both trepidation and exhilaration washed over them. The enigma of the AI-driven stock had drawn them into a world of intrigue and danger, but they were determined to see their mission through to the end. The world was about to change, and the battle for truth would leave no one unscathed.

The Revelation

The world held its breath as Jason Reeves and Sarah Reynolds watched the progress bar inch closer to completion. The evidence they possessed, a damning exposé of The Syndicate's manipulation and deceit, was about to be broadcast to the world. The enigma of the AI-driven stock, which had drawn them into a world of intrigue and danger, was on the verge of being unmasked.

In the dimly lit safehouse, the tension was palpable. The sound of their own breathing seemed deafening as they waited for the data to be transmitted to servers around the globe. The consequences of their actions were uncertain, and the shadow of The Syndicate loomed over them.

As the progress bar reached 100%, a sense of exhilaration washed over Jason and Sarah. The evidence was out, and the world would soon know the truth that had remained hidden for far too long. But there was no time for celebration—the battle for truth had only just begun.

Within moments, news outlets around the world began to report on the revelations contained in the stolen data. The Syndicate's secrets were laid bare for all to see—manipulation of financial markets, orchestration of global crises, and a sinister plan known as Project Phoenix that sought to reshape the global economy.

THE REVELATION

The world reacted with shock and disbelief. Financial markets trembled, and governments scrambled to respond. The Syndicate's influence was far-reaching, and the fallout from their actions threatened to destabilize economies and institutions.

But The Syndicate was not about to go quietly into the night. As the world's attention turned to the revelations, they launched a counteroffensive—a campaign of disinformation and propaganda designed to discredit Jason, Sarah, and the evidence they had uncovered.

The battle for truth had become a war of narratives, and the lines between fact and fiction blurred. The world was divided, and the fate of the AI-driven stock hung in the balance.

In the midst of the chaos, Jason received a cryptic message from an anonymous source—a whistleblower from within The Syndicate who had grown disillusioned with their actions. The source claimed to have information that could expose the enigma of the AI-driven stock once and for all.

Jason and Sarah knew that they couldn't ignore the source's message. The enigma had led them on a treacherous journey, and the truth remained just out of reach. They had to follow this lead, no matter the risks.

The meeting took place in a dimly lit alleyway, far from the prying eyes of The Syndicate. The source was a shadowy figure, their identity concealed beneath layers of disguise. Their voice was a whisper in the darkness, and their words carried the weight of revelation.

"The enigma of the AI-driven stock is not just about manipulation," the source said, their voice tinged with urgency. "It's about control—control over governments, economies, and the fate of nations. The Syndicate's ambitions go far beyond Wall Street."

Jason and Sarah listened in awe as the source revealed a hidden world of corporate espionage, political manipulation, and economic warfare. The Syndicate's influence extended to the highest levels of power, and their reach was global.

But the source had a revelation that would change everything. They possessed evidence of a secret project known as "Aegis." It was a plan to use the AI-driven stock to exert control over the world's financial systems, to reshape the global economy according to The Syndicate's whims.

With this evidence in their possession, Jason and Sarah knew that they had the key to unmasking the enigma of the AI-driven stock once and for all. The battle for truth had reached a new level, and the consequences of their actions were immeasurable.

But The Syndicate was not about to back down. They launched a relentless campaign to track down Jason, Sarah, and the whistleblower. The world had become a dangerous place, and their every move was scrutinized.

As they moved from one safehouse to another, always one step ahead of their pursuers, Jason and Sarah knew that they were running out of time. The enigma of the AI-driven stock had drawn them into a world of intrigue and danger, and the shadows seemed to close in with every passing moment.

Their journey took them to the heart of the financial district, where they discovered the existence of a hidden network of activists and hackers who shared their mission. These digital warriors possessed the skills and knowledge to breach The Syndicate's defenses and expose the truth.

The plan was set in motion—a coordinated cyberattack that would reveal the evidence of Project Aegis to the world. The stakes were impossibly high, and the consequences of failure were dire. But Jason and Sarah knew that they had to see their mission through to the end, to unmask the enigma of

THE REVELATION

the AI-driven stock and bring The Syndicate to justice.

As they watched the progress bar inch forward, a sense of trepidation and exhilaration washed over them. The enigma had led them to this pivotal moment, a moment that would test their resolve and reshape the fate of the financial world.

With the evidence secure, they initiated the release. The information would be broadcast to the world, unmasking The Syndicate's secrets and revealing the extent of their manipulation. The consequences would be far-reaching, and the world would soon know the truth that had remained hidden for far too long.

But as the upload completed, a feeling of unease settled over them. The shadows seemed to close in, and the world outside was a blur of lights and shadows. The enigma of the AI-driven stock had brought them to the precipice of history, and the battle for truth had left them in its relentless grip.

The Final Confrontation

The city was engulfed in a cacophony of sirens and flashing lights as news of The Syndicate's secrets spread like wildfire. The revelations contained in the stolen data had sent shockwaves through the financial world, and the world awaited their next move.

Jason Reeves and Sarah Reynolds had unmasked the enigma of the AI-driven stock, exposing The Syndicate's manipulation and deceit to the world. But their actions had not gone unnoticed, and The Syndicate was closing in.

In a hidden safehouse on the outskirts of the city, Jason and Sarah watched as the world reacted to their revelations. Financial markets trembled, governments scrambled to respond, and the battle for truth raged on.

But The Syndicate was not about to go quietly into the night. They launched a relentless campaign to discredit Jason, Sarah, and the evidence they had uncovered. The world was divided, and the fate of the AI-driven stock hung in the balance.

As they monitored incoming messages on secure communication channels, a cryptic message arrived from an anonymous source—a whistleblower within The Syndicate who had grown disillusioned with their actions. The source claimed to have information that could expose the enigma of the AI-driven stock once and for all.

THE FINAL CONFRONTATION

Jason and Sarah knew that they couldn't ignore the source's message. The enigma had led them on a treacherous journey, and the truth remained just out of reach. They had to follow this lead, no matter the risks.

The meeting took place in the dead of night, in a clandestine location far from the city's prying eyes. The source was a shadowy figure, their identity concealed beneath layers of disguise. Their voice was a whisper in the darkness, and their words carried the weight of revelation.

"The enigma of the AI-driven stock is not just about manipulation," the source said, their voice tinged with urgency. "It's about control—control over governments, economies, and the fate of nations. The Syndicate's ambitions go far beyond Wall Street."

Jason and Sarah listened in awe as the source revealed a hidden world of corporate espionage, political manipulation, and economic warfare. The Syndicate's influence extended to the highest levels of power, and their reach was global.

But the source had a revelation that would change everything. They possessed evidence of a secret project known as "Aegis." It was a plan to use the AI-driven stock to exert control over the world's financial systems, to reshape the global economy according to The Syndicate's whims.

With this evidence in their possession, Jason and Sarah knew that they had the key to unmasking the enigma of the AI-driven stock once and for all. The battle for truth had reached a new level, and the consequences of their actions were immeasurable.

But The Syndicate was not about to back down. They launched a relentless campaign to track down Jason, Sarah, and the whistleblower. The world had become a dangerous place, and their every move was scrutinized.

As they moved from one safehouse to another, always one step ahead of their pursuers, Jason and Sarah knew that they were running out of time. The enigma of the AI-driven stock had drawn them into a world of intrigue and danger, and the shadows seemed to close in with every passing moment.

Their journey took them to the heart of the financial district, where they discovered the existence of a hidden network of activists and hackers who shared their mission. These digital warriors possessed the skills and knowledge to breach The Syndicate's defenses and expose the truth.

The plan was set in motion—a coordinated cyberattack that would reveal the evidence of Project Aegis to the world. The stakes were impossibly high, and the consequences of failure were dire. But Jason and Sarah knew that they had to see their mission through to the end, to unmask the enigma of the AI-driven stock and bring The Syndicate to justice.

As they watched the progress bar inch forward, a sense of trepidation and exhilaration washed over them. The enigma had led them to this pivotal moment, a moment that would test their resolve and reshape the fate of the financial world.

With the evidence secure, they initiated the release. The information would be broadcast to the world, unmasking The Syndicate's secrets and revealing the extent of their manipulation. The consequences would be far-reaching, and the world would soon know the truth that had remained hidden for far too long.

But as the upload completed, a feeling of unease settled over them. The shadows seemed to close in, and the world outside was a blur of lights and shadows. The enigma of the AI-driven stock had brought them to the precipice of history, and the battle for truth had left them in its relentless grip.

THE FINAL CONFRONTATION

In the days that followed, the world reacted to the revelations with shock and disbelief. Financial markets trembled, and governments launched investigations into The Syndicate's actions. The enigma of the AI-driven stock had been unmasked, and the consequences were far-reaching.

But The Syndicate was not about to go down without a fight. They launched a counteroffensive, a campaign of disinformation and propaganda designed to discredit Jason, Sarah, and the evidence they had uncovered. The world remained divided, and the battle for truth raged on.

As Jason and Sarah moved from one safehouse to another, they received a message from an anonymous source—a message that contained a chilling revelation. The source claimed to have evidence that The Syndicate had discovered the identity of the whistleblower who had provided them with the information about Project Aegis.

The whistleblower was in grave danger, and time was running out. Jason and Sarah knew that they had to find and protect the source before The Syndicate could silence them forever.

Their search led them to a remote location on the outskirts of the city, a hidden safehouse where the whistleblower had gone into hiding. But when they arrived, they found the safehouse abandoned, the evidence of a struggle evident.

The enigma of the AI-driven stock had led them to this final confrontation, a battle for truth and justice that had pushed them to the limits of their courage. The world was watching, and the fate of the whistleblower hung in the balance.

With determination in their hearts, Jason and Sarah followed a trail of clues that led them deeper into the heart of The Syndicate's operations. The shadows seemed to close in around them, but they were determined to see their mission through to the end.

As they reached the heart of The Syndicate's lair, a hidden office within a seemingly innocuous corporate building, they were met with a chilling sight. The whistleblower, battered and bruised but alive, was held captive by members of The Syndicate.

The leader of The Syndicate, a formidable figure known only as "The Architect," stood before them, a sinister smile on their face. The Architect had orchestrated this final confrontation, and the enigma of the AI-driven stock had drawn them all into its relentless grip.

"You may have exposed our secrets," The Architect said, their voice dripping with menace. "But you will not escape this place alive."

The battle that ensued was fierce and relentless. Jason and Sarah fought with every ounce of their strength, determined to protect the whistleblower and bring The Syndicate to justice. The Architect and their henchmen were formidable adversaries, and the outcome of the confrontation was uncertain.

But in the end, it was a combination of wit, determination, and sheer willpower that allowed Jason and Sarah to emerge victorious. The Architect was captured,

and The Syndicate's operations were exposed for all to see.

As they stood amidst the ruins of the hidden office, the enigma of the AI-driven stock finally unmasked, a sense of triumph and relief washed over Jason and Sarah. The battle for truth had been won, and justice had prevailed.

But the enigma of the AI-driven stock had left its mark on them. The journey had tested their resolve and pushed them to the limits of their courage. The world had been forever changed, and the battle for truth had left no one unscathed.

In the days that followed, The Syndicate's operations were dismantled, and its members brought to justice. The world began to heal from the shockwaves of the revelations, and financial markets regained their stability.

Jason and Sarah, their mission complete, looked out at the cityscape from a quiet rooftop, the enigma of the AI-driven stock finally behind them. The world below pulsed with life, and the future held promise and uncertainty in equal measure.

As they embraced the dawn of a new day, they knew that their journey had been one of discovery and revelation, a journey that had tested their resolve and pushed them to the limits of their courage. The enigma of the AI-driven stock had drawn them into a world of intrigue and danger, but they had emerged on the other side, unmasking the hidden manipulators and bringing them to justice.

The world had changed, and the enigma had been laid to rest. But Jason and Sarah knew that the battle for truth was ongoing, and they would continue to stand on the side of justice, no matter the challenges that lay ahead.

The Aftermath

In the aftermath of the final confrontation with The Syndicate, Jason Reeves and Sarah Reynolds found themselves in a world transformed. The enigma of the AI-driven stock had been unmasked, and the battle for truth had left an indelible mark on their lives.

As they stood on the rooftop, overlooking the cityscape bathed in the soft hues of dawn, they felt a sense of relief and closure. The enigma had drawn them into a world of intrigue and danger, but they had emerged victorious, unmasking the hidden manipulators and bringing them to justice.

But the journey had taken its toll. The world below pulsed with life, and the future held promise and uncertainty in equal measure. Jason and Sarah knew that their mission was far from over, and the battle for truth was ongoing.

In the days that followed, the world began to heal from the shockwaves of the revelations. Financial markets regained their stability, and governments launched investigations into The Syndicate's actions. The fallout from their manipulation was far-reaching, and the world had learned a painful lesson about the dangers of unchecked power.

Jason and Sarah, their mission complete, found themselves in the spotlight of media attention. They were hailed as heroes and whistleblowers, individuals who had risked everything to expose The Syndicate's secrets. But with the

THE AFTERMATH

accolades came scrutiny, and their lives were no longer their own.

The enigma of the AI-driven stock had left a trail of destruction in its wake, and there were those who sought to blame Jason and Sarah for the chaos that had ensued. They became targets of anger and resentment, individuals who had disrupted the status quo and threatened the balance of power.

As they navigated the complexities of their newfound fame, Jason and Sarah remained vigilant. The battle for truth was ongoing, and they knew that there were powerful interests who would stop at nothing to protect their secrets.

But they were not alone in their mission. The underground network of activists and hackers who had supported them throughout their journey continued to operate in the shadows, dedicated to exposing corruption and injustice. It was a world where truth was a precious commodity, and the risks were immeasurable.

One day, as Jason and Sarah were attending a clandestine meeting with their underground allies, they received a message—a message that contained a cryptic warning. The enigma of the AI-driven stock had not been fully unraveled, and there were still secrets waiting to be discovered.

The message led them to a hidden archive of data, a treasure trove of information that had eluded them until now. It was a labyrinth of encrypted files and confidential documents, a digital maze that held the answers to the remaining mysteries of The Syndicate's operations.

With determination in their hearts, Jason and Sarah embarked on a new journey, a quest to uncover the remaining secrets of the enigma. The world had changed, but the battle for truth was far from over.

Their journey took them to the darkest corners of the financial world, where danger lurked at every turn. They encountered adversaries who were determined to protect The Syndicate's secrets, individuals who would stop at nothing to silence them.

But Jason and Sarah were not easily deterred. The enigma of the AI-driven stock had drawn them into a world of intrigue and danger, and they had emerged stronger and more resolute than ever. The battle for truth was their calling, and they would see it through to the end.

As they delved deeper into the hidden archive, they uncovered evidence of a new plot—a plan known as "Operation Phoenix Rising." It was a sinister scheme to resurrect The Syndicate's influence and continue their manipulation of financial markets.

The evidence was damning, and it revealed a network of individuals who were determined to rebuild The Syndicate's empire. The consequences of their actions could be catastrophic, and the world remained oblivious to the impending threat.

With the evidence in their possession, Jason and Sarah knew that they had a duty to expose the new plot and protect the world from The Syndicate's resurgence. The battle for truth had taken them on a journey of discovery and revelation, and they were determined to see it through to the end.

But the path ahead was treacherous, and the dangers that awaited them were real. The enigma of the AI-driven stock had drawn them into a world of shadows and secrets, and the battle for truth would leave no one unscathed.

As they prepared to confront the new threat, they couldn't help but reflect on the journey that had brought them to this point. The enigma had tested their resolve and pushed them to the limits of their courage, but it had also shown them the power of truth and the importance of standing on the side of justice.

THE AFTERMATH

The world below continued to pulse with life, and the future remained uncertain. But Jason and Sarah were determined to face the challenges that lay ahead, to unmask the remaining secrets of the enigma, and to protect the world from those who sought to manipulate it.

As they stood on the precipice of a new chapter in their mission, they knew that the battle for truth was ongoing, and they would continue to stand on the side of justice, no matter the risks or obstacles that lay in their path. The enigma of the AI-driven stock had drawn them into a world of intrigue and danger, but it had also shown them the power of determination and the resilience of the human spirit.

Operation Phoenix Rising

The darkened room was bathed in the bluish glow of computer screens, casting an eerie light on Jason Reeves and Sarah Reynolds as they delved deeper into the hidden archive of data. The enigma of the AI-driven stock had led them on a relentless quest for truth, and they had uncovered evidence of a new plot—the sinister "Operation Phoenix Rising."

As they scanned through the encrypted files and confidential documents, the enormity of the new threat became clear. The remnants of The Syndicate were determined to rebuild their empire and continue their manipulation of financial markets. It was a plot that could have catastrophic consequences, and the world remained oblivious to the impending danger.

With each passing moment, the urgency of their mission weighed heavily on Jason and Sarah. The evidence they had uncovered was damning, and they knew that they had a duty to expose the new plot and protect the world from The Syndicate's resurgence.

But the path ahead was treacherous, and the dangers that awaited them were real. The enigma of the AI-driven stock had drawn them into a world of shadows and secrets, and the battle for truth had exacted a toll on their lives. Yet they were determined to see their mission through to the end.

In the dimly lit room, Sarah's fingers danced across the keyboard as she worked to decrypt a particularly challenging file. It was a race against time, and every second counted. The world outside continued to pulse with life, unaware of the impending threat that loomed.

As Sarah made progress, a voice echoed through the room—the voice of an unexpected intruder. The door creaked open, and a figure stepped into the room, their face obscured by the shadows.

"You've come far, but you won't go any further," the intruder said, their voice dripping with menace.

Jason and Sarah spun around to face the newcomer, their hearts pounding in their chests. The enigma of the AI-driven stock had drawn them into countless confrontations, and they knew that this could be their most dangerous yet.

The intruder's features slowly became visible as they stepped further into the room—a henchman of The Syndicate, a loyal servant of their nefarious cause. They were armed, their weapon glinting in the dim light, and their eyes bore the cold determination of an adversary who would stop at nothing to protect The Syndicate's secrets.

"We know what you've uncovered," the henchman continued, their voice laced with contempt. "Operation Phoenix Rising will succeed, and there's nothing you can do to stop it."

Jason and Sarah exchanged a knowing glance. The enigma had brought them face to face with danger on numerous occasions, but they had always relied on their wits and determination to prevail. This time would be no different.

With a quick nod, they sprang into action. Sarah's fingers danced across the keyboard as she continued to decrypt the files, determined to uncover every detail of Operation Phoenix Rising. Jason, on the other hand, moved with the agility and precision of someone who had faced danger before.

The henchman advanced, their weapon pointed at Jason and Sarah. The stakes were high, and the room seemed to close in around them as they engaged in a deadly game of cat and mouse.

But Jason and Sarah had the advantage of surprise. With a swift motion, Jason hurled a nearby computer monitor at the henchman, causing them to stumble and lose their grip on the weapon. Sarah seized the opportunity, leaping forward to disarm their adversary.

A struggle ensued, with Jason and Sarah working in tandem to subdue the henchman. It was a battle of strength and will, with the outcome uncertain. The enigma of the AI-driven stock had prepared them for moments like these, and they fought with the determination of individuals who had faced danger head-on.

Finally, with a well-timed maneuver, they managed to disarm the henchman and subdue them. The room fell silent, the tension in the air dissipating as the threat was neutralized.

Breathing heavily, Jason and Sarah looked at each other, a sense of relief washing over them. The enigma had tested their resolve and pushed them to the limits of their courage, but they had prevailed once again.

With their adversary captured and immobilized, they returned to their mission. The decrypted files revealed the full extent of Operation Phoenix Rising—a plan to infiltrate financial institutions, manipulate stock prices, and create a new era of financial chaos.

The evidence was damning, and Jason and Sarah knew that they had to act quickly to expose the plot and protect the world from The Syndicate's resurgence. The battle for truth was far from over, and the consequences of their actions were immeasurable.

As they prepared to leave the room, they received a cryptic message on a secure communication channel—an anonymous source who claimed to have information about The Syndicate's leadership. The source offered to meet in person, to provide them with the final piece of the puzzle.

Jason and Sarah knew that they couldn't ignore the source's message. The enigma of the AI-driven stock had brought them face to face with danger and intrigue, and they had a duty to see their mission through to the end.

The meeting took place in a remote location, far from the city's prying eyes. The source was a shadowy figure, their identity concealed behind layers of disguise. Their voice was a whisper in the

darkness, and their words carried the weight of revelation.

"I know who leads The Syndicate," the source said, their voice tinged with urgency. "Their identity will shock the world, and their plans go far beyond Operation Phoenix Rising."

Jason and Sarah listened in awe as the source revealed the name of The Syndicate's leader—a figure known only as "The Puppetmaster." The Puppetmaster's identity had remained hidden for far too long, and the consequences of their actions were immeasurable.

But the source had more to reveal. They possessed evidence of The Puppetmaster's involvement in a global conspiracy—a plan to use the AI-driven stock to exert control over governments, economies, and the fate of nations.

With this evidence in their possession, Jason and Sarah knew that they had the key to unmasking the ultimate enigma—the identity of The Syndicate's leader and the extent of their manipulation. The battle for truth had reached its climax, and the world awaited their next move.

With determination in their hearts, they initiated the release of the evidence. The information would be broadcast to the world, exposing The Puppetmaster's secrets and revealing the true enigma that had remained hidden for far too long.

But as the upload progressed, a feeling of unease settled over them. The shadows seemed to close in, and the world outside was a blur of lights and shadows. The enigma of the AI-driven stock had brought them to the precipice of history, and the battle for truth had left them in its relentless grip.

As they watched the progress bar inch forward, they knew that the world was about to change. The enigma had led them on a journey of discovery and revelation, and they were determined to see their mission through to the end, to expose The Puppetmaster's true identity and bring them to justice.

The world below continued to pulse with life, unaware of the impending revelation that would shake its foundations. The enigma of the AI-driven stock had drawn Jason and Sarah into a world of intrigue and danger, but they were determined to stand on the side of justice, no matter the challenges or risks that lay ahead.

www.ingramcontent.com/pod-product-compliance
Lightning Source LLC
LaVergne TN
LVHW050027080526
838202LV00069B/6944